Sister Sister!
Book Log Journal

Other Journals by Shelia E. Bell
"Journal Your Way Through It"

Get more Info About Shelia E. Bell books!

Sister Sister!

Book Log Journal

Shelia E. Bell

"Reading gives us someplace to go when we have to stay where we are."

The ideal tool and log for avid readers, book clubs, bloggers, and more. Keep up with the books you've read. Make notes for future virtual or in person book discussions. Keep a list of your favorite and least favorite authors and book titles. "Sister Sister! Book Log Journal" is your personal journal to all things literary.

BOOK OF THE MONTH

BOOK TITLE	
AUTHOR(S)	

MY NOTES & DISCUSSION QUESTIONS

_____
_____
_____
_____
_____
_____
_____
_____
_____
_____
_____
_____
_____
_____
_____
_____
_____
_____
_____
_____
_____
_____
_____
_____
_____

"Reading gives us someplace to go when we have to stay where we are."

BOOK TITLE	
AUTHOR(S)	

MY NOTES & DISCUSSION QUESTIONS

_____
_____
_____
_____
_____
_____
_____
_____
_____
_____
_____
_____
_____
_____
_____
_____
_____
_____
_____
_____
_____
_____
_____
_____

"Reading is to the mind what exercise is to the body."

"Books are a uniquely portable magic."

BOOK TITLE	
AUTHOR(S)	

MY NOTES & DISCUSSION QUESTIONS

"Reading gives us someplace to go when we have to stay where we are."

BOOK TITLE	
AUTHOR(S)	

MY NOTES & DISCUSSION QUESTIONS

_____
_____
_____
_____
_____
_____
_____
_____
_____
_____
_____
_____
_____
_____
_____
_____
_____
_____
_____
_____
_____
_____
_____

"Reading is to the mind what exercise is to the body."

"Books are a uniquely portable magic."

BOOK TITLE	
AUTHOR(S)	

MY NOTES & DISCUSSION QUESTIONS

_____
_____
_____
_____
_____
_____
_____
_____
_____
_____
_____
_____
_____
_____
_____
_____
_____
_____
_____
_____
_____
_____
_____
_____
_____

"Reading gives us someplace to go when we have to stay where we are."

BOOK TITLE	
AUTHOR(S)	

MY NOTES & DISCUSSION QUESTIONS

_____
_____
_____
_____
_____
_____
_____
_____
_____
_____
_____
_____
_____
_____
_____
_____
_____
_____
_____
_____
_____
_____
_____
_____
_____
_____

"Reading is to the mind what exercise is to the body."

BOOK TITLE	
AUTHOR(S)	

MY NOTES & DISCUSSION QUESTIONS

_____
_____
_____
_____
_____
_____
_____
_____
_____
_____
_____
_____
_____
_____
_____
_____
_____
_____
_____
_____
_____
_____
_____
_____
_____
_____

"Reading gives us someplace to go when we have to stay where we are."

BOOK TITLE	
AUTHOR(S)	

MY NOTES & DISCUSSION QUESTIONS

_____
_____
_____
_____
_____
_____
_____
_____
_____
_____
_____
_____
_____
_____
_____
_____
_____
_____
_____
_____
_____
_____
_____
_____
_____

"Reading is to the mind what exercise is to the body."

"Books are a uniquely portable magic."

BOOK TITLE	
AUTHOR(S)	

MY NOTES & DISCUSSION QUESTIONS

_____
_____
_____
_____
_____
_____
_____
_____
_____
_____
_____
_____
_____
_____
_____
_____
_____
_____
_____
_____
_____
_____
_____
_____
_____
_____
_____

"She read books as one would breathe air, to fill up and live."

"Reading gives us someplace to go when we have to stay where we are."

BOOK TITLE	
AUTHOR(S)	

MY NOTES & DISCUSSION QUESTIONS

_____
_____
_____
_____
_____
_____
_____
_____
_____
_____
_____
_____
_____
_____
_____
_____
_____
_____
_____
_____
_____
_____
_____
_____
_____
_____

"Reading is to the mind what exercise is to the body."

"Books are a uniquely portable magic."

BOOK TITLE	
AUTHOR(S)	

MY NOTES & DISCUSSION QUESTIONS

_____
_____
_____
_____
_____
_____
_____
_____
_____
_____
_____
_____
_____
_____
_____
_____
_____
_____
_____
_____
_____
_____
_____
_____

"She read books as one would breathe air, to fill up and live."

"Reading gives us someplace to go when we have to stay where we are."

BOOK TITLE	
AUTHOR(S)	

MY NOTES & DISCUSSION QUESTIONS

_____
_____
_____
_____
_____
_____
_____
_____
_____
_____
_____
_____
_____
_____
_____
_____
_____
_____
_____
_____
_____
_____
_____
_____
_____

"Reading is to the mind what exercise is to the body."

BOOK TITLE	
AUTHOR(S)	

MY NOTES & DISCUSSION QUESTIONS

_____
_____
_____
_____
_____
_____
_____
_____
_____
_____
_____
_____
_____
_____
_____
_____
_____
_____
_____
_____
_____
_____
_____
_____
_____

"Reading gives us someplace to go when we have to stay where we are."

BOOK TITLE	
AUTHOR(S)	

MY NOTES & DISCUSSION QUESTIONS

_____
_____
_____
_____
_____
_____
_____
_____
_____
_____
_____
_____
_____
_____
_____
_____
_____
_____
_____
_____
_____
_____
_____
_____
_____

"Reading is to the mind what exercise is to the body."

"Books are a uniquely portable magic."

BOOK TITLE	
AUTHOR(S)	

MY NOTES & DISCUSSION QUESTIONS

_____

_____

_____

_____

_____

_____

_____

_____

_____

_____

_____

_____

_____

_____

_____

_____

_____

_____

_____

_____

_____

_____

_____

_____

_____

"She read books as one would breathe air, to fill up and live."

"Reading gives us someplace to go when we have to stay where we are."

| BOOK TITLE | |
| AUTHOR(S) | |

MY NOTES & DISCUSSION QUESTIONS

_____
_____
_____
_____
_____
_____
_____
_____
_____
_____
_____
_____
_____
_____
_____
_____
_____
_____
_____
_____
_____
_____
_____
_____
_____

"Reading is to the mind what exercise is to the body."

"Books are a uniquely portable magic."

BOOK TITLE	
AUTHOR(S)	

MY NOTES & DISCUSSION QUESTIONS

_____
_____
_____
_____
_____
_____
_____
_____
_____
_____
_____
_____
_____
_____
_____
_____
_____
_____
_____
_____
_____
_____
_____
_____
_____
_____

"She read books as one would breathe air, to fill up and live."

"Reading gives us someplace to go when we have to stay where we are."

BOOK TITLE	
AUTHOR(S)	

MY NOTES & DISCUSSION QUESTIONS

_____
_____
_____
_____
_____
_____
_____
_____
_____
_____
_____
_____
_____
_____
_____
_____
_____
_____
_____
_____
_____
_____
_____
_____
_____
_____
_____

"Reading is to the mind what exercise is to the body."

"Books are a uniquely portable magic."

BOOK TITLE	
AUTHOR(S)	

MY NOTES & DISCUSSION QUESTIONS

"Reading gives us someplace to go when we have to stay where we are."

BOOK TITLE	
AUTHOR(S)	

MY NOTES & DISCUSSION QUESTIONS

_____
_____
_____
_____
_____
_____
_____
_____
_____
_____
_____
_____
_____
_____
_____
_____
_____
_____
_____
_____
_____
_____
_____
_____
_____

"Reading is to the mind what exercise is to the body."

BOOK TITLE	
AUTHOR(S)	

MY NOTES & DISCUSSION QUESTIONS

_____
_____
_____
_____
_____
_____
_____
_____
_____
_____
_____
_____
_____
_____
_____
_____
_____
_____
_____
_____
_____
_____
_____
_____

"Reading gives us someplace to go when we have to stay where we are."

BOOK TITLE	
AUTHOR(S)	

MY NOTES & DISCUSSION QUESTIONS

_____
_____
_____
_____
_____
_____
_____
_____
_____
_____
_____
_____
_____
_____
_____
_____
_____
_____
_____
_____
_____
_____
_____
_____
_____
_____

"Reading is to the mind what exercise is to the body."

"Books are a uniquely portable magic."

BOOK TITLE	
AUTHOR(S)	

MY NOTES & DISCUSSION QUESTIONS

"Reading gives us someplace to go when we have to stay where we are."

BOOK CLUB LOG

My Favorite Book Club Reads And Recommendations

1. _____
2. _____
3. _____
4. _____
5. _____
6. _____
7. _____
8. _____
9. _____
10. _____
11. _____
12. _____
13. _____
14. _____
15. _____
16. _____
17. _____
18. _____
19. _____

"Reading is to the mind what exercise is to the body."

"Books are a uniquely portable magic."

20. _____
21. _____
22. _____
23. _____
24. _____
25. _____
26. _____
27. _____
28. _____
29. _____
30. _____
31. _____
32. _____
33. _____
34. _____
35. _____
36. _____
37. _____
38. _____
39. _____
40. _____

"She read books as one would breathe air, to fill up and live."

"Reading gives us someplace to go when we have to stay where we are."

Hosted Book Club Authors

Hosted Author	Book Discussed	Date

"Reading is to the mind what exercise is to the body."

"Books are a uniquely portable magic."

My Favorite Authors

1. _____

2. _____

3. _____

4. _____

5. _____

6. _____

7. _____

8. _____

9. _____

10. _____

My Favorite Nonfiction Books

1.

2.

3.

4.

5.

6.

7.

8.

9.

10.

My Favorite Fiction Books

Favorite Novels or Fiction Books

1. _____

2. _____

3. _____

4. _____

5. _____

6. _____

7. _____

8. _____

9. _____

10. _____

My *To Be Read* (TBR) List

1. _____
2. _____
3. _____
4. _____
5. _____
6. _____
7. _____
8. _____
9. _____
10. _____
11. _____
12. _____
13. _____
14. _____
15. _____
16. _____
17. _____
18. _____

"Books are a uniquely portable magic."

19. _____
20. _____
21. _____
22. _____
23. _____
24. _____
25. _____
26. _____
27. _____
28. _____
29. _____
30. _____
31. _____
32. _____
33. _____
34. _____
35. _____
36. _____
37. _____
38. _____
39. _____
40. _____

"She read books as one would breathe air, to fill up and live."

"Reading gives us someplace to go when we have to stay where we are."

My Reading Notes

_____

_____

_____

_____

_____

_____

_____

_____

_____

_____

_____

_____

_____

_____

_____

_____

_____

_____

_____

_____

"Reading is to the mind what exercise is to the body."

My Reading Notes

My Reading Notes

_____

_____

_____

_____

_____

_____

_____

_____

_____

_____

_____

_____

_____

_____

_____

_____

_____

_____

_____

_____

My Reading Notes

My Reading Notes

_____

_____

_____

_____

_____

_____

_____

_____

_____

_____

_____

_____

_____

_____

_____

_____

_____

_____

_____

_____

My Literary Events

Literary events, book signings, book club events, festivals, I plan to attend

Literary Event	Date/Time	Location (Virtual or In-Person)

"Reading gives us someplace to go when we have to stay where we are."

Other books by Shelia E. Bell
(Some titles may still be found under former name Shelia Lipsey)

Young Adult Titles
House of Cars
The Life of Payne
The Lollipop Girl
The Righteous Brothers

Standalone Novels
Show A Little Love (*out of print*)
Always Now and Forever Love Hurts
Into Each Life
Sinsatiable
What's Blood Got To Do With It?
Only In My Dreams
The House Husband
Cross Road
Forever Ain't Enough

Series Books
Beautiful Ugly
True Beauty

Adverse City Series
The Real Housewives of Adverse City
The Real Housewives of Adverse City 2
The Real Housewives of Adverse City 3
The Real Housewives of Adverse City 4

Anthologies
Bended Knees
Weary to Will
Learning to Love Me
Show A Little Love (I)

"Reading is to the mind what exercise is to the body."

"Books are a uniquely portable magic."

My Son's Wife Series
My Son's Wife: The Beginning (Book 1)
My Son's Ex-Wife: Aftershock (Book 2)
My Son's Next Wife (Book 3)
My Sister My Momma My Wife (Book 4)
My Wife My Baby...And Him (Book 5)
The McCoy's of Holy Rock (Book 6)
Dem McCoy Boys (Book 7)
My Brother, Father...And Me (Book 8)
My Truth, My Time, My Turn (Book 9)
Dem Folk at Holy Rock (Book 10)

Holy Rock Chronicles
Calling Dr. Daniels
The Woman in Apartment 3D

Nonfiction
A Christian's Perspective: Journey Through Grief
How To Live Your Life Like Its Golden:
Even When There is No Pot of Gold at the End of the Rainbow

Journals
Journal Your Way Through It
Sister, Sister Book Log Journal

"She read books as one would breathe air, to fill up and live."

"Reading gives us someplace to go when we have to stay where we are."

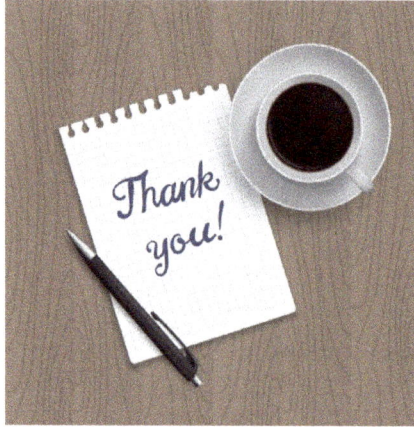

Contact sheliawritesbooks@yahoo.com
Visit www.sheliawritesbooks.com to learn about
other books and literary services!

Follow me on Amazon bit.ly/sheliabell

"Reading is to the mind what exercise is to the body."

"Books are a uniquely portable magic."

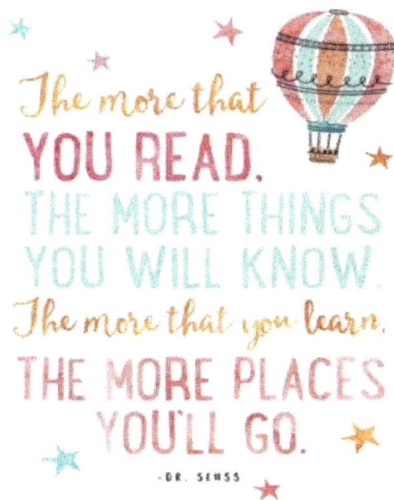

The more that
YOU READ,
THE MORE THINGS
YOU WILL KNOW.
The more that you learn,
THE MORE PLACES
YOU'LL GO.
-DR. SEUSS

"She read books as one would breathe air, to fill up and live."